28 Day *Novel Writing* Challenge

M.H. Salter

Daytime Moon Publishing

Published by Daytime Moon Publishing, South Australia

Excerpts from *Dove* by M.H. Salter 2016

Excerpts from *A Rose By Any Other Name* by M.H. Salter 2016

eBook ISBN: 978-0-9925267-6-4
Print Book ISBN: 978-0-9925267-7-1

Contact the author at the.excited.writer.is@gmail.com

Others In This Series by M.H. Salter

28 Day Characters Challenge
28 Day Story Structure Challenge
28 Day First Chapter Challenge
28 Day Endings Challenge

*

Fiction Books by M.H. Salter

Doorways
Dove
A Rose By Any Other Name

*

Non-Fiction Books by M.H. Salter

Peter Tork: Words of Wisdom From A.A. to ZEN
Davy Jones: Words of Wisdom From A.A. to ZEN

Introduction

Hello, Writer!

Welcome to this 28 Day Challenge for writers struggling to complete their novel's first draft, or needing to up-level their existing manuscript, by working through the daily lessons and writing exercises around character development, story structure, the first chapter, and publishing options.

Aside from the physical act of writing, this challenge has a second purpose. One that is even more important. It is designed to inspire and motivate you, and most importantly to increase your belief in yourself as an artist. If you don't already consider yourself a "writer" or an "artist", then I have news for you: the fact that you are either considering this challenge — or have already signed up for it — proves that you *are* a writer because you are aiming to improve on your craft. That in itself shows that you consider yourself, and your artistic merits to be worthy.

According to science, it takes an average of 21 days to form a new habit by implementing a daily practice. It takes a following 90 days to make it into a permanent lifestyle change. This 28 Day Challenge is designed to help you incorporate writing time into your life in order for it to become routine. Over these 28 days you will learn to make yourself and your writing a priority, carve out a daily routine that can become a habit, and lead you toward a MS of which you will be proud and excited to put out into the waiting world.

In the *Novel Writing Challenge*, you will receive a daily lesson focusing on a different aspect of novel writing:
  • character development, character arc, character types, and theme
  • story structure, story arc, conflict and pace, and how to deal with writer's block
  • the first chapter, hooks, first and last lines, and the use of backstory
  • the final chapter, publishing options, pitches, synopsis and cover letters
  • getting excited and staying excited about your work-in-progress

So many of us will start a project, get about a third of the way through, and stop. I believe writing a novel is a cumulative process. You need to gather enough momentum (ie. excitement) at the beginning, so that when you hit those downhill slumps of self-doubt and writer's block, you will have enough inertia to get you through to actually completing your first draft. Each of these 28 day writing challenges will help you to get and stay excited about your work-in-progress.

Each daily practice contains simple, bite-sized snippets and exercises that you can either ponder on for the day and make some notes before bed, or just do in a few minutes over your morning coffee, so that even those of us who can't find time to write can still get something out of it. At the end of the 28 days, even if you only spent ten minutes per day on a challenge, you will end up with *four and a half hours* of writing time that you wouldn't have completed ordinarily. If you only manage a hundred words a day, by the end of the challenge you'll be *2,800 words down*! That's basically a chapter a month if you keep it up.

Remember, with this challenge, you will only get out what you put in. Allow yourself just ten minutes a day. Invest in yourself.

These daily lessons and exercises are taken from my book: *The Excited Writer.* Once this challenge is complete, you are invited to purchase the full book for even more lessons and exercises, take up another 28 Day Challenge in a more specific area, or even opt to work with me one-on-one via an assessment or mentorship.

Remember, a habit takes an average of 21 days to form, and a following 90 days to become a permanent lifestyle change. Whether you finish one 28 day course and start another right away, or just continue on your own, please keep up the daily routine — even just ten minutes a day — because you are worth it.

This challenge may not have you completing your novel in 28 days, that is not the point of it. The point, my friend, is to carve out for you a new daily habit. I am honoured to be a part of your personal writing journey. Thank you for including me on the ride!

Warm regards,
Melanie Hyland Salter
(M.H. Salter)

Day One: Introduction to Characters

Characters are what make your novel readable. They are the bait with which we draw in the readers. Your characters, therefore, need to be interesting and relatable. Over this next week we will be learning more about your characters — mainly what they *want*, and what they *need* (because these two things are very different) — and the journey of transformation they are about to undergo.

Every character in your story will be embarking on a transformative journey. Every significant character will be somehow different by the time they get to the end of the book. They will start off internally wounded, and end up healed. All thanks to you.

But first, who are your main characters? Aside from their name, gender, ethnicity, etc, who *are* they beneath all those labels? The labels will certainly create a two-dimensional portrait, but we want them pop out in full 3D. To do that, they need to have underlying beliefs, fears, superstitions, addictions, hopes, dreams, and so on…

Let me ask you this: you know a fair bit about your main character, but what *don't* you know about them?

Exercise: 5 min

Your main character's world is about to change. They are standing on the precipice.

How do they feel about their current situation?
What are they afraid of?
What are they confidant about?
What do they think they will learn on this journey?
What do they want most in the world?
What would they sacrifice to achieve this?

<u>Set a timer for five minutes.</u>

Either write a dialog between yourself and your main character, or have your character write a private journal entry, expanding on the above questions, and any others you come up with.

Don't think too hard, just write in a stream-of-consciousness style and see what pours out of them.

Keep going until the timer is up or until they surprise you with a hidden truth.

When you are finished, edit and reshape it into a scene. Insert this scene somewhere in your book.

Feel free to keep going and do this for all your main characters.

Day Two: Theme

Today we are looking at theme.

Theme is what people really mean when they say, 'Oh, you're writing a book? Cool! What's it about?'

The real answer to this question has nothing to do with genre or plot lines. It has to do with the ultimate lesson all the characters will learn. It has to do with a universal core value.

All books have a theme. And so does yours. You may even have uncovered it during yesterday's exercise. What was it your character wanted more than anything? This is usually their *physical* desire, the tangible thing they believe will fix all their problems. It won't though. What will truly heal them is something they don't realise they *need*: an emotional goal. And this is usually an intangible equal to their physical goal. It is your character's core value.

And *this is the theme* of your book.

An example of a core value is self worth, self love, freedom, integrity, compassion, creativity, security, honesty, spirituality. The list could go on and on.

If your book has a strong theme based on a core value then it has resonating potential to a high volume of readers.

The theme of the book needs to be visible, not just in your storyline, but in *each* of your characters. They should *all* have the same core value — this is their underlying motivation. It is what drives their decisions and fuels their belief systems. But it also keeps your book in alignment.

Theme is a powerful tool for any writer, as it also comes with the ability — if harnessed correctly — to avoid long battles with writers block, or the dreaded "sagging middle" syndrome. If you can use your theme in every single scene you write, this will then give *every single scene* you write a *reason* to be included in the book. It will give you something to focus on when you are stuck. It will keep your book on the right path without wandering off aimlessly for a few chapters.

Theme is a compass to your lesson, to your climax, to your ending, to a full and fast-paced character transformation.

Theme is the ultimate lesson of the story, something your reader will take away with them once they have turned the last page.

<u>Author Examples</u>

In my book, *Dove,* the theme is freedom.

Opposing viewpoints of freedom could be: control, captivity, force, imprisonment, restraint

The story takes place around the draft and the Vietnam War, which allows the reader to see how characters can view the concept of freedom differently. Some want to fight for it actively by going to war, some want to fight for it passively by avoiding the war. It provides two sides to a universal theme, and the reader will unknowingly be challenged throughout the book, and eventually come out the other side with a new view on this topic.

Let's look at freedom of choice, for example. In 1970, with the draft for induction into the armed forces, freedom of choice was taken away. Some chose to defy this and dodge the draft by going "underground" or leaving the country at the risk of arrest if they were ever caught. They attempted to take back control in this way and keep their freedom.

Another example during this era was freedom to dissent. This was challenged when, during an anti-war protest at Kent State University, four students were shot by the National Guard, a true event that the fictional characters in *Dove* witness. The US Government attempted to restrain the youth of America from voicing their opinions.

During the war, physical freedom was literally taken away when soldiers were captured as prisoners of war. This focuses on captivity as an opposition to freedom.

So you can see how theme, and its opposing viewpoints, were used to create conflicting plot lines.

<u>**Exercise: 5 min**</u>

Let's work out your theme.

Question: Oh, you're writing a book? Cool! What's it about? No… What is it *really* about? What is the core value within your story? What life lesson do your characters need to learn?

Answer: _________________________
Theme: _________________________

Write down two opposing viewpoints with which this core value can be contrasted in your book.

Opposing Viewpoint 1: _____________________
Opposing Viewpoint 2: _____________________

For each opposing viewpoint, write down arguments for and against (these will be used in tomorrow's challenge).

Day Three: Character Development

We come into this world with clean slates and we are moulded or programmed by the beliefs and actions of those who raised us or who influenced our lives. Our culture, traditions, celebrations, traumas, phobias, even unintentional lessons we may have picked up empathically from our parents all become lodged deep below the surface of ourselves and contribute to the ways we view and react to the world around us. What is safe and unsafe? What is good and bad? What is right and wrong? What is tolerable and unacceptable?

It is said that by the age of seven, we have completely developed this unique programming (no two people are the same). Certain beliefs have been formed and imprinted upon us. In a lot of cases, however, these controlling beliefs within our psyches are simply not true. Let me say that again: *Certain beliefs have been formed and imprinted upon us. In a lot of cases, however, these controlling beliefs within our psyches are simply not true.* Unfortunately though, because these false beliefs exist on a subconscious level, we remain totally unaware of them. The only ways in which we acknowledge them, are in the negative reactions we might have to certain situations, and even then, these reactions feel normal. Why? Because that is how we were programmed to react.

How does this relate to character development?

Every memorable character is memorable because the reader was able to relate to them on a subconscious level. And the reason for this is because the character was not perfect. None of us in the real world are perfect, so why should your characters be?

Your character has these subconscious beliefs too, and the journey toward overcoming them is what will create their transformational journey, or in other words, their character arc.

Throughout the story, these false beliefs need to be challenged one by one, and unlearned. Their core wound is in direct opposition to the character's core value (theme), which we learned in the previous day's exercise.

To sum up so far, your character has a core wound and a false belief system that exists deep in their subconscious. If they ever want to achieve happiness, they need to heal this core wound. Their core wound, and false beliefs have all led your character to developing certain character flaws that prevent them from living their best life. As your characters move from point A to point Z over the course of their story, their beliefs will be challenged over and over again in different ways, until they are ultimately overcome, and proven to be false, thus transforming your characters, completing their arcs, and healing their core wound.

<u>Exercise: 15 min</u>

1. Write out a list of possible false beliefs your character has and needs to overcome throughout their journey. (Remember these beliefs need to relate to the core value and opposing viewpoints you came up with yesterday. These beliefs are somehow preventing them from reaching their goal.)

Example: *I'm not good enough to write a book. I don't have enough time. No one will be interested in this topic anyway.*

2. How can each false belief be challenged at different points throughout your story to finally make your character realise this belief is *not* true?
Example: *They start a 28 Day Writing Challenge and see that they are able to get scenes written in a short amount of time.*

3. What positive/true belief will they be able to replace the false ones with, and thus take a step closer to being healed?

Example: *Books are subjective and appeal to different people. There will always be someone interested in what I write. I can schedule time every day to write.*

Day Four: Character Types – Protagonist (The Good Guy)

Today we will look at the protagonist. The good guy.

As we have already established, every character is on their own transformational journey. To put this another way: every character is the protagonist in their own mind. (Even the bad guys.) And every character therefore has their own individual character arc, which we will look at briefly today.

Yesterday we looked at your character's internal flaw, which is being constantly reinforced by their false beliefs. But how exactly do we get them to overcome these beliefs? Well, just like real life, it's all based on *desire*. No one ever aspires to change unless there is something they *want* and don't yet have.

Now, in your protagonist's life, there is something that they *want*. Badly. It is the one thing they believe that, if they can obtain, will make them happy, or complete, or fulfilled in life. This is the goal that drives your story. It is the main plot of the book. This is your answer whenever someone asks you: "Oh, you're writing a book? Great? What happens in it?" It is what your character will spend most of the next few hundred pages hunting for, and trying to achieve.

Why?

Because it is the thing they believe will cure their internal flaw (whether they are aware of the flaw or not). And it must be something they can physically *do*, or tangibly *hold*, so that it is easily recognised by the reader that the goal has been achieved. Because, spoiler alert, once the protagonist does achieve this goal, they will suddenly realise that it *isn't* actually what they *need* at all.

What they actually *need* is an emotional goal, something within themselves.

Exercise: 5-10 min

Fill out this basic character arc template for each of your main characters, making each one the protagonist in their own individual arc.

At the start of the book…

- This character is unhappy because of _________________ (Core Wound)

- They believe the only thing that can heal them and solve their current problem is _____________________ (Physical Want)

- They will remain stuck in their unhappiness because they believe the following things about themselves: __________________ (False beliefs)

- Once they have unlearned these beliefs, they will realise the only thing that can actually heal them, and solve their current problem, is __________________ (Emotional Need)

- Once they achieve this emotional need, they will finally be in alignment with their core value _________________ (theme).

…End of the book

Day Five: Character Types – Antagonist (The Bad Guy)

The antagonist is the character who will try to prevent the hero from succeeding in their goals. Your antagonist is not necessarily the "villain" of the story, they are the character who has the *same desire* as the hero.

The antagonist wants the exact same physical goal as your protagonist and will thwart your hero, again and again, in their own quest for success. This is what makes them an antagonist. It is not that they want the *opposite* goal to the hero… they want the *same* goal, and only one of them can succeed.

Remember, the antagonist is the protagonist in their own head, even if they do seem to be the "bad guy" as far as the reader is concerned. So you, as the author, must now employ *empathy*. This will allow the reader to (in some way at least) want the antagonist to succeed as well.

Now sometimes, your story may not have an actual villain. Some stories have circumstance or fate as the opposing force, rather than a particular character — a metaphorical antagonist. If this is the case, then you need to create a character who will *metaphorically represent* this antagonistic force. Give this character scenes in which they can explore both sides of the book's theme, and give them a journey that allows sympathy to creep in. If you can do this, not only will you create a character who has many layers, but you will also create more conflict for your protagonist if they are confronted with *a desire to forgive.*

Author Example

In my novel *Dove*, Japhy (Protagonist) seeks his own freedom by avoiding the draft into the Vietnam War. As a pacifist, Japhy must either illegally resist his induction to the Vietnam War, or join the army and become a soldier. The American Government (Antagonist) also seeks Japhy's freedom by taking away his choices and thwarting his escape from the draft. The US Government is not exactly an easy antagonist to portray in a book. So, let me introduce you to (Uncle) Sam. A frat boy who is literally red, white and blue — red hair, white skin, blue eyes. When we first meet him, Sam (referred to in the beginning as Red Hair) is a detestable guy who, along with his friends, physically

assaults Japhy and sexually assaults Ray, and there is
absolutely nothing that Japhy can do about it. Beneath
the surface though, we see a faint glimmer of humility
when Sam explains his reasons for believing the war in
Vietnam is not only necessary, but good.

"Innocent?" Red Hair looked at me with pupils the size of
plates. "Don't you watch the news? Those Gooks ain't
innocent!"

"They're just as innocent as our side are!" I said.

"North Viet Nam are nothing but communist bullies!" said
Red Hair. "If we don't make a stand against them, and help
defend South Viet Nam, our country could be taken over by
communism as well. It's the Domino Effect. You should be
thanking us! We are fighting for your freedom! For peace!"

I crossed my arms. "Oh, don't give me that line. Fighting
for peace! It's bullshit! It's the biggest oxymoron there is.
People are dying and you are defending it!"

"Yes, I'm defending it," said Red Hair. "I think this war is
good, but not because people are dying over there. It's good
because we are helping other people to live."

Later in the novel, (spoiler alert) Japhy meets up with
Sam again. He confronts Sam about the attack and
finally delivers the punch to the face he's been dreaming
of. But not only does Sam not defend himself against
Japhy, he goes on to elicit sympathy and forgiveness.

When I finally sit, Sam leans in and whispers, "Listen, I want you to know how bad I feel about what I did." He winces and rubs his jaw. "Was your old lady okay?"

"What do you care?"

"That's what I'm trying to tell you. What we did to you two that day ... it haunts me. I've never done anything like that before; I was high on speed, so I wasn't in control of myself." He holds up his hands and says quickly, "Not that it's an excuse. It isn't. The other guys were always bragging to me about how many girls they'd balled. I know I'm not much of a looker, so I felt ... I don't know, like I had to prove to them I wasn't a loser. I hate myself for what I did, and I don't expect you to forgive me, or even believe me, but I just want you to know that I'm sorry. I'm a good guy, I really am. We all make mistakes, do things we regret, things we have to deal with, and live with, for the rest of our lives."

I shake my head at him and look away.

"I understand how you must feel, seeing me again like this, and I understand if you can't forgive me, but can we put it behind us?" He holds out his hand to me again. "So, what do you say?"

Anger bubbles my skin. Singes up through my limbs, into my torso, converging into one huge wave that flows into my brain. My head throbs. I can't believe what I've just heard and I am so angry I could spit. But I am not angry at Sam. I flex my aching knuckles and I think again of the crunch as my fist hit his jaw, but I do not feel the warm glow of satisfaction I'd expected. This is the jerk who attacked Ray. This is the monster whose face I once dreamed about putting through a window. This is a human who shows utter remorse. And I hate him for that. But I hate myself more for wanting to forgive the son-of-a bitch.

So whether your antagonist is metaphorical or actual, give them a human soul that the reader will connect with. Make them humble, remorseful, and on some small level forgivable. Show the reader there may be a possibility that this character could turn their life around, even if it is completely unlikely, because the reader will always cheer on a character who wants to change.

Exercise: 10 min

1. What is your protagonist's physical desire (core value)? _______________

2. Which character (or characters) in your story also wants this for themself, and needs to prevent your protagonist from achieving this goal? (Can be more than one if metaphorical). This person is your Antagonist. Antagonist: _________________

3. Give your antagonist some empathy. Choose someone in the real world that you do *not* like. Now think of four traits that you do like about this person.

Dig deep if you have to — remember this person has friends and family that love them, so they must have *some* good qualities. Write a scene where your antagonist displays these positive traits, or does something nice. Insert this scene into your story.

Day Six: Character Types – Ally (The Inspirational Guy)

There will come a point in your story where everything has gone wrong and your protagonist hits rock bottom. They finally realise that the one thing they've been seeking, in order to heal them, isn't what they actually need. Enter, the ally.

The ally is the one character who will rise up at the last minute and inspire your hero to succeed when it all seems hopeless. The ally is the only one who is able to force your protagonist to face their internal flaw, see their core wound, and begin to heal it by finally seeking the emotional goal. They can be your protagonist's best friend that has been alongside them for the entire journey, or they can be a pop-up character that appears in one chapter specifically to deliver this lesson to your protagonist.

Remember, each character — even the minor ones — is the star of their own story: they are their own protagonist, they have their own antagonist, and their own ally. Each character will therefore relate to the other characters in different ways, and these relationships will all weave together to form a complex and rich tapestry in your story. Each role is different but necessary for the character arc to be completed.

<u>Exercise: 5 min</u>

<u>Set a five minute timer.</u>

Write a short paragraph about the book's theme. Why have you chosen this topic? Why is it important to you? Why should it be important to the reader? What do you want the reader to learn because of your book?

Edit this paragraph into a powerful and inspiring speech. Insert it into your book right before the climax, where your protagonist's ally can this message with as much force as possible.

Day Seven: Character Conclusions

If you've just gone a full week of writing every day, filled out your character profiles, and taken a huge step in fleshing out your current work in progress, well friggin' done! I am *so* proud of you.

And if you maybe missed a few lessons, or not completed the exercises, that's okay too; these practices aren't going anywhere and you can go back to any one of them whenever you want. I am still so proud of you, because you are still here, and you are still showing up for yourself!

Remember, however fast or slow you go is okay. Congratulate yourself for being here in the first place.

Today, we are wrapping up our look into characters by writing out their basic character arcs. Once you have these in place, you will have a strong foundation for each one. This can help to prevent writers block by clarifying directions and decisions that the characters will need to make in further scenes.

In summary of this week, each character (protagonist, antagonist and ally) is the star of their own story. They each have a core wound, a physical desire, and an emotional need that relates directly to your book's theme. They are their own protagonist, they have their own antagonist, and their own ally. Each character will relate to the other characters in different ways, and these relationships will all weave together to form a complex and rich tapestry in your story. Each role is different but necessary for the character arc to be completed.

Exercise: 10 min

Using the points we have already looked at over this week, fill out your character arc cheat sheet. For this exercise, look at all of your characters as the protagonist of their stories, and give each of them their own individual arc, antagonist and ally.

Protagonist: ______________
Core Value: ______________
Opposing viewpoint: ______________________
Core Wound: ____________________

Physical want (physical representation of core value):

____

____

Emotional need (emotional representation of core
value):

____

____

False Beliefs to overcome: ____________________________

____

____

____

Antagonist: _______________
Physical want: _________________

Ally: _______________
Lesson to deliver/theme stated): ________________

Day Eight: Introduction to Structure

Full disclosure, I used to be a pantser. That is, until I started looking into the art of structure and story arc, and it appealed to me.

In case you don't know what the hell I am talking about, a "pantser" is a writer who writes by the seat of their pants. A "plotter", by comparison, is a writer who writes out the plot before they start writing the book itself.

So which is the right way? Plotter or pantser? There *is* no right or wrong way. Whichever way appeals to you personally, that is *your* right way and either one works well.

Most pantsers (my former self included) avoid looking into structuring their novel for fear of being boxed in by the rigid plot lines they may set themselves. They may feel like their creative juices are stifled by the rules of the structuring process. But this is simply not true; planning a story structure is completely different than planning a plot.

The Story structure is based on *The Hero's Journey*, by Joseph Campbell. This is where your book is broken down into Act One, Act Two, Act Three.

When creating your story structure, you may need to know your character's goals and flaws (which we discussed last week). This enables you to know what the characters are aiming for, and the beliefs they have that need to be challenged. (You don't necessarily need to go about it in this order, ie character and then structure — this is just what works for me, personally. You can work on story structure first, and use that to build up your characters. Again, whatever works for you.)

Today I want to look at your writing style. Do you consider yourself to be a plotter or a pantser? Or maybe a little of both?

Exercise: 15 min

Discover the Pantser Magic. If you are a plotter, sit down and start writing a scene "by the seat of your pants". Just let the character be the leader. Let them surprise you. Let them tell you exactly *why* they want their physical desire, and keep writing until they reveal something to you that you had not expected. This the pantser magic, where the writer feels that jolt of, 'Whoa, I did not see that one coming!'

Discover the Plotter Power. If you are a pantser, sit down, and write a scene in which your main character is thinking about their physical goal, the thing they desire most, the thing they believe will save them (even though *you*, as the god-like creator, already know that it won't.) This is the omnipotent power of a plotter. Keep writing this scene, infusing it with subtle hints foreshadowing the character's future disappointment.

If you are both, do both exercises.

Edit and insert this scene somewhere into your work-in-progress.

Day Nine: Story Arc

Either way, plotter or pantser, you will end up with a story arc, and this is what we will be looking at today.

The story arc is where you break everything down into three acts and 15 beats. These 15 beats can be seen in almost all novels. Even if you are unaware of them, you have probably subconsciously incorporated them already.

<u>1. Opening Image</u>
This is a paragraph-length snapshot, most likely in the first page of your book, possibly using metaphor or symbolism, that gives the reader an idea of who the character is at the beginning. (This image will be directly contrasted at the end of the book against a final image). Remember, a picture is worth a thousand words.

<u>2. Theme Stated</u>
In this beat, your theme (or main character's emotional need) is literally spelled out to your character. They disregard it completely.

3. The Normal World

This is the life your characters live before the story kicks into gear and their world is turned upside-down This is where you briefly introduce the main characters and hint at the problems that need to be addressed, whether the characters are aware of them or not.

4. The Inciting Incident

Sometimes referred to as the catalyst, this is the point where your characters' lives are interrupted by something BIG. It disrupts their normal life, and prevents the character from being able to continue living life the way they previously were.

5. Debate

Because of the inciting incident, your characters will find themselves at a fork in the road, and will be forced to make a decision. Either way, from this point, their lives will never be the same again.

6. Act Two Begins

Because of the debate, your characters have made their choice, and will have been somewhat changed as a result. They begin their journey toward a physical goal they believe will fix everything.

7. The Upside-down World

Having started along the path toward this new goal, the character usually meets up with a new set of characters who will help (or hinder) them on their journey.

8. Fun and Games

This is essentially the premise of the book, and shows how your character plans to achieve their physical goal, and the steps they must take to do so.

9. Midpoint (The Second Inciting Incident)

Plot twist. Something BIG happens to interrupt everything, and basically turns things upside-down again. This is usually the point where the main character finally achieves their physical goal only to realise it isn't what they believed it to be, or the character hits rock bottom and realises they can *not* achieve the physical goal after all.

It is a second inciting incident.

This should be unexpected, yet probable, and of course, completely devastating to all involved. This will force the character to question the physical goal they believed they wanted to achieve.

10. Everything Hits the Fan

This is the downward spiral. Everything starts to go wrong. This can take place either in the external world, with antagonistic characters thwarting the protagonist at every turn, or in the internal world, with the protagonist self-sabotaging themself and destroying their own progress via bad choices over and over again.

11. Death

This is where the character experiences the death of their own flaw. They finally let it go. They overcome their false belief system. Their old, flawed self dies.

12. The Awakening

Because of the death, the character reflects on what they have learned, on how the life lesson or theme needs to be attained, and is now reborn into a new version of themselves, with a new determination and a new emotional goal.

13. Act Three Begins
The newly awakened character makes a plan on how to achieve this new emotional goal.

14. Climax
The character makes a last ditch effort to achieve their emotional goal, and they either succeed or fail (depending on your genre). Conflict and tensions rise to this final, ultimate peak. The highest peak in the story. The climax. Everything has been leading up to this one major confrontation. Someone will win, and someone will lose.

15. Resolution
Your characters pick up the pieces of their lives (if they came out alive, that is). This beat contains a closing image, a new metaphorical snapshot of the book's theme that shows how the character has changed, and how life will be now. It should contrast against the opening image. This is where the loose ends are tied, and the reader says goodbye.

Exercise: 15 min

Fill out the story arc template for your work-in-progress:

1. The Opening Image

2. Theme Stated

3. The Normal World

4. The Inciting Incident

5. The Debate

6. Act Two Begins

7. The Upside-down World

8. Fun and Games

9. Midpoint

10. Everything Hits the Fan

11. Death

12. The Awakening

13. Act Three Begins

14. Climax

15. Resolution

Throw yourself a few curveballs.

Whether you have a completed draft, or if you are brainstorming it all right now, write out your entire story arc using this template on a separate sheet of paper. Now, close your eyes, and mark *three* points at random, and write in the exact opposite of whatever is taking place. The first choice is usually the safe choice, the predictable choice. Would this new plot line improve your story?

Day Ten: Conflict

So, once you have implemented all your ideas for the story arc, you have to make sure that every page (yes, every single page!) on this curved line is an interesting page. The only way to do this is with conflict. If the story arc is the bricks of your books, then conflict is the mortar that glues everything together.

Conflict can be seen as the good guy battling with the bad guy, that's just a given. But in this case — and in terms of a structural tool that is going to enhance your book tenfold — I am referring to one character who is battling their internal *self*.

Every character has something they desperately want, and this is where we dive deep and use these desires to our advantage. It is now your job as the writer, as the godlike-writer and omnipresent masochist that you are, to analyse what this desire is. To work out what the exact *opposite* of this desire would be. And to then work out how the hell this character can also want that opposite desire just as badly. This is where your delicious conflict will come from.

Conflict can be shown in the form of inner turmoil (guilt, fear, indecisiveness, etc.) or it can be from external forces (arguments, fate, weather conditions, etc.) And the best way to create impact is to have both of these forces working against each other at the same time.

Let me state this again: Your characters' conflict must be present, in some form, on every page. Yes, I understand that this might mean a hell of a lot of work, a lot of rewrites, but writing a great novel is not easy and does not happen overnight.

Author Example

The book *Dove* opens with the female narrator, Ray, hitchhiking to Canada with her boyfriend, Japhy, to escape his draft into the army and the Vietnam War. (The arrival of his draft letter is The Inciting Incident). Ray has given up her whole world in order to go with Japhy, and obviously, the thing she wants most at this point is for him to reach the border and safely avoid the draft. Yet, she keeps catching herself guiltily wishing she could stay in the USA, and go to university, and make something of her life.

Likewise, Japhy, a pacifist, doesn't want to fight, kill, or die — hence the reason he is heading for the border. However, knowing innocent people are being injured and killed in Vietnam, and that if he joins the army perhaps he could save some of these people, makes him want to go and fight. He then feels guilty and cowardly for running away. These inner conflicts are the basis of every scene in the first half of my novel.

Exercise: 10 min

1. Take a few of your main characters and for each one write a list of their main five desires. (These will most likely be the plot and subplots of your book.)

2. For each desire, write down its exact opposite.

3. Write some notes as to how your character can justify also wanting that opposite desire at the same time.

4. Choose one character and one set of opposing desires. Write a scene in which your character struggles with this internal conflict. Insert this scene into your work in progress.

Day Eleven: Pace

Pace is all about keeping the reader turning pages. Aside from creating conflict on every page, which we covered previously, another way is by making sure all your scenes, or chapters, or sections, or even paragraphs, start and end with a *bang!*

You know what it's like: you're tired and you tell yourself, "I'll just finish this chapter." But the chapter ends in such a way that you simply have no choice but to go to the next chapter. So you think, "Okay, I'll read the first line just to see what is about to happen." But the first line hooks you in again. Next thing you know you're in the middle of that chapter, and and you tell yourself, "I'll just finish this chapter." And once again, that chapter ends in such a way that you simply have no choice but to go to the next chapter. Next thing you know, the sun is coming up, you haven't slept a wink, and you end up finishing the entire book.

Pace is all about creating a delicate dance, the one-two step of the first and last lines that continue to carry the reader away, and then finding that magic balance with the crescendo and the climax, and positioning your chapter break right between those two peaks.

<u>Exercise: 15 mins</u>

If you have completed a first draft, take a sheet of paper and write out each chapter's first and last lines. Make sure they are each intriguing in their own right. If any seem to lack punch, rewrite them. Spend time on each one to make sure it packs a punch.

If you don't have a completed draft yet, go through your basic outline. Brainstorm a chapter outline. Place your chapter endings in the middle of the rising crescendoes, and begin the next chapter with the climax you were building up to.

<u>Author Example: *Dove*</u>

Chapter 1. Ray POV
Fear can inspire you to fight, or to fly, in order to survive a threat. We flew.
...
The car shuddered to a stop in a sunlit clearing as bright as the fear in the Japhy's eyes, and all three frat boys turned to face me.

Chapter 2. Japhy POV
All three frat boys turn and face Ray with hungry-wolf
smiles and full-moon eyes.

...

A boot connects with my exposed face and I feel the edges
of my world flicker and start to fade again.

Chapter 3. Ray POV
In the dirt beneath Red Hair I twisted and kicked and
scratched and punched until I was free from his grip and up
and running and surrounded by trees and all alone.

...

Whatever you have planned for Japhy – I sent my thought
out to this new day – you will have to break through me to
get to him; you will have to break me to pieces.

Author Example: *A Rose By Any Other Name*

Prologue
Destiny swirls and plinks inside my crystal ball like a moth
against a window, eager to break free and influence the
future of the soul to whom it is attached.

...

But my crystal ball does not break; it simply bounces,
unharmed, unaltered, and rolls back to me, stopping at my
bare toes.

Chapter 1

Orlando Starre is perched on a lookout, facing a cliff, towards which he is about to drive as fast as he can without stopping.

...

Shifting his focus to the reflection of his own eyes, and to the hope that is also visible there, he wonders exactly which outcome he is hoping for.

Chapter 2

The tattooist is not what Ben Starr expects to see when he enters the studio: puny with orange hair, freckled skin, thick-lensed glasses and a cute cartoon Pegasus tattoo on his skinny shoulder.

...

"And what?" asks Orlando. "You think carving her name into your flesh with ink is going to magically make her want cock? Sorry, man, but it ain't gonna happen. Trust me, I'm going to help you forget this chick, or die trying!"

Chapter 3

Shepherd Rose watches his neighbour, Guy Shylock, nodding along to the story; his elbows rest on the desk, his head propped in his hands, his eyes wide and enthusiastic as a toddler's at a magic show.

...

He looks at this grinning kid, this God damned son of a bitch, this businessman to whom he's just essentially sold his only daughter, and Shepherd Rose prays for a God damned miracle.

Day Twelve: Emotion

Most stories are character driven, not plot driven (unless it's a whodunnit). Therefore, the best way to hook a reader is with empathy through the character.

All stories are written to convey emotion in the reader. But how often is this actually achieved? One mistake that many writers make is to try and convey a certain emotion by *describing* that emotion. They think that by simply describing the character *feeling* a certain way that the reader will automatically feel that way too. But this is not necessarily the case.

To really smack your readers in the face with an emotional fist, you need to catch them off guard. If your main character has just been left at the altar and is crumpled on the floor in a soggy ball of tears, it is unlikely that your reader will also be sobbing into the pages of the book. Why? Because sorrow is an expected response for a character to feel in this particular situation, and subconsciously, your reader will be prepared to protect themselves from it.

You need to sneak up on your reader and throw an emotion at them they are not expecting.

One way to achieve this effect is to go sideways.

Going sideways is where you come at the reader from a completely unexpected direction.

Look at the emotion that your character is feeling in the particular scene you are working on. This is usually the expected emotion, the automatic response.

Now turn this around and do the exact *opposite* of that emotion.

Author Example

In *Dove*, there is a moment where a young girl witnesses the death of a baby. You would imagine that the emotion felt here would be horror and shock. But in order to convey these feelings, I had to take it sideways to a whole different level and catch them both — the character and the reader — off guard using an unexpected emotion.

My father carries her past the twelve year-old me in the hallway. Red-faced, he runs with her, his keys jingling in his pocket. They jingle like reindeer bells on a sleigh. And that's when I start laughing. I just start fucking laughing. [She] is dead, and it's Christmas Eve, and it's all my fault, and I'm laughing like the horrific monster I've become.

By using *laughter* in this scene, rather than tears or racing hearts or clenched stomachs, it makes the character feel disgusted in herself, because surely only a truly horrible person would laugh at a terrible time like this. And surely, this revelation is something that the reader would have to agree with. So by coming in from a completely different direction with the emotional punch, the reader is left shocked and horrified after all, even though they had probably believed they had safely blocked that blow.

Exercise: 15 min

Pick an emotional scene in your book, or write a scene to insert.

Look at the emotion that your character is feeling. This is usually the expected emotion, the automatic response.

Now turn this around and do the exact *opposite* of that emotion.

Write, or rewrite this scene using this new emotion.

Day Thirteen: Writer's Block

I believe that Writer's Block is simply another way of saying: *lack of inspiration*. For example, if you are feeling bored with your story, or you come to an indecision about what will happen next, then you have hit the dreaded wall. So in theory, if you are suffering from Writer's Block, then all you need to do in order to break down the wall is to get excited about your story again.

Exercise: 15 min

Tap into that feeling of budding love you had when you first started thinking about this story idea.

1. Write down the reason you decided to start this particular storyline. What made you decide that this story needs to be written?

2. How did you feel when the inspiration about this story first struck you? Write a random scene that brings out this feeling in you again.

3. Take the scene you are stuck on and analyse it as if you are writing an essay.

What is happening in this scene and why?

What needs to happen next and why?

Note: the *WHY* part of this analysis is the most important part. If you can't come up with a good answer for needing to incorporate this scene, then that in itself may be your answer. Maybe it is not as important in the overall story as you thought? Maybe you need to scrap that idea and move on because this scene is blocking you from moving forward.

Day Fourteen: Structure Conclusion

You've made it to the two-week mark! Well done. How do you feel? You are now officially half way to making writing a daily practice for life.

This week was all about incorporating more conflict and tension in your book, which therefore leads to a faster paced story that a reader will have trouble putting down.

Today is an integration day. Being our last day on structure before we move into a different topic, I want you to integrate what you have learned and spend the time writing on your work in progress to enhance the pace, conflict and tension.

It's all well and good to read books on structure and pace, and to learn about increasing tension and conflict, but unless you actually put this into practice and integrate it into you writing style, it will drop away.

Set a timer for 15 minutes and write a new scene that incorporates inner conflict with your character.

Increase the pace by ending this scene with a *bang!* Can this be used as a chapter ending?

Day Fifteen: First Impressions Introduction

Welcome to week three! Look at you go! I'm so proud of you for making time for yourself throughout this challenge. Take a moment right now to look back at the amount of work you have done on your work-in-progress throughout this challenge so far. However much you have done, give yourself credit — it's more than you would have done otherwise, right? And that is something to be proud of.

Okay, now that we have looked at your characters and your basic plot, this week we will be looking at the first impression that your book will have on a reader. This is conveyed through different hooks in the first line and first paragraph, as well as the last line of the first chapter.

Remember, the first chapter is the first impression the reader will have, not only of your writing, but also of your story and your characters. It needs to grab hold, grab hold quickly, and grab hold fiercely.

This week we will either start writing your first chapter, or revising your already-written first chapter (depending on what stage you're at.)

Today though, I want to look at first lines in general.

Exercise: 15 min

Go to your bookshelf and take down five of your favourite novels.

Look at each one of their first lines.

Does it hook you right away? If yes, Why? If no, Why not?

Why are these sentences so appealing to you, personally? Or not appealing? What worked and what didn't?

Let the reasons for this appeal simmer away within you until tomorrow…

Day Sixteen: First Line

The first line of a good novel is like that spark you get when you meet the person you will love. It is the pick-up line. It is the wink of an eye. It is that wonderful rush of possibility beating in your bloodstream, throbbing with the thought: *is this it, is this it, is this it?*

There are a few techniques in which great first lines grab hold and won't let go:

Imagery.
Like a barbed hook through a fleshy cheek, a vivd image pierces your reader's soft skin, lifts them thrashing from the safety of their sofas, drags them helpless and screaming and breaking their nails across the floor until they are pulled into a world from which they may never return, whole, again.

Voice.
If your character is, indeed, a *character* — someone intriguing and unusual and entertaining (and of course, they obviously *are*, I mean, *rolls eyes* for the sake of crap, why else would you be bothered to write about them in the first place if they were just as dull and

unmentionable as, well, the reader!) — use their unique
voice to attract your reader and set the tone for the rest
of the book.

Surprise!
A good shock in the first line is a wonderful way to
keep the reader intrigued. You want the reader to think,
"Huh?" or "What the hell does that mean?" and the
secret to carrying out this technique is to write
something unexpected, unusual, quirky, fantastical, or
even nonsensical. Write a beginning that will cause the
reader's eyebrows to lift right off their face, because in
your novel, this may very well happen.

Humour.
They say laughter is the best way to feel comfortable
with something or someone. So why not use it for this
first meeting between your reader and your character?
Open your novel with a funny polar bear, it's a great ice
breaker.

Philosophy.
Make the reader *think*. Better yet, go deeper and make
the reader think, "What would I do if this were *me*?"
Inside the pages of every wonderful novel is a deep,

universal truth, and therefore a fearful realisation that anything can happen to any of us at any time.

<u>Exercise: 10 min</u>

1. If you already have a first chapter, what type of first line technique have you used: imagery, voice, surprise, humour, philosophy.

If you haven't written it yet, which of these above techniques appeals to you?

2. Write at least three new first lines using different techniques. Do any of these work better as your opening line?

Day Seventeen: First Paragraph

So, as we discussed yesterday, you need to engage your reader like you would a potential lover. The best way to do this is to ask a question they need answered. It could be as simple as, "Why is this girl sad?" or as complex as, "How far will this character go to save a loved one ... and what the hell would *I* do in this situation?"

A great unanswered question in your first paragraph will keep a reader turning pages. (Tip: keep that question unanswered for as long as possible.)

The first paragraph needs to be relevant to the story itself. It needs to give the reader a subtle hint of what type of story they are about to embark on: comedy, drama, tragedy, horror. But alongside this, the first paragraph needs to hint at the theme of the book, and the transformational journey that is likely to follow, using an emotional pull.

This emotional pull is what should hook your reader the most. It should grab their hearts and refuse to let go. It should be strong, intense, and immediate. And the best way to do this is with *primal emotion* such as fear, anger, sadness, surprise, trust, joy, anticipation, disgust, etc.

Author Example

In the first paragraph of *Dove*, a sense of urgency is built around the concept of fear, and the different ways people react to it (fight or flight response).

   Fear can inspire you to fight, or to fly, in order to survive a threat. We flew. We flapped our wings as hard and as fast as we could to escape the country that wanted to kill us. And with every down-stroke, I prayed we weren't leaving a trail of white feathers in our wake.

Fear is used here for two reasons. Reason one, it lets the reader know the characters are frightened, are running from something deadly, and are concerned about being followed. This makes the reader curious to find out what the characters are running from. And reason two, it makes the reader question what *they* would do in the same situation, which makes the story relatable — if the reader feels this could easily happen to them, they become emotionally invested in the character's outcome.

<u>**Exercise: 15 min**</u>

1. On a sheet of paper, write out your entire first paragraph (or a few of them if they are short).

2. In that paragraph, circle three words or phrases that convey a sense of urgency, or intrigue, and relate to a primal emotion. (If you can't find three, write down three words or phrases that convey for you a sense of urgency, and insert these into your first paragraph.)

3. During at least three separate points throughout your first chapter, insert these circled words/phrases again. Build each one into a paragraph that will further highlight the question, sense of urgency, or intrigue you established in your first line.

Day Eighteen: Backstory

Backstory is everything that has happened to your character prior to your first chapter. Backstory is the reason why your character is starting his or her story in the exact place where chapter one begins. Backstory is the reason why your character is the way they are. Backstory gives your characters depth. The full Backstory should NOT appear anywhere in chapter one. Ever. Because backstory will — funnily enough — take the reader *back*. Therefore the story will no longer move *forward,* and that is something you must avoid until the inertia of your plot is well-established.

Author Example

In the first chapter of *Dove,* Ray alludes to a piece of her backstory that the reader will not learn until Chapter 47. But up until this revelation, the story is sprinkled with crumbs of curiosity in order to draw out the tension of her deadly secret.

Of course, I'd never told [Japhy] about what I'd done. He didn't know that my soul was shredded. He didn't know that killing someone rips a hole right through you. And if I have anything to do with it, he will never know how it feels to have somebody else's death ingrained into your very being, as much a part of who you are as is your blood cells and eyelids and yesterdays. [...] They say that killing during war is heroic, but you can't mend a shredded soul with a war medal. I knew about these things. And because I knew about them, I would make sure that Japhy never had to; his soul will stay as pure and white as mine had been, once upon a time.

Give your characters secrets. Secrets that they plan to never reveal to anyone. Secrets that are eating them up on the inside, and therefore peppering their journey with spicy little tidbits and hints of true inner conflict.

Make the backstory of every character deep and complex so that these secrets, and what they eventually reveal, will effect the character's decisions in relation to the story plot.

Exercise: 15 min

1. Delete any backstory from your first chapter, but leave a small hint of it, and why this character is conflicted because of it, without saying what it actually is.

2. Plan ways to sprinkle backstory in over the course of a few chapters. Tease the reader with it! Dangle the carrot as long as you can, and then a little longer, and a little longer …

Day Nineteen: Last Line

We covered this slightly in Day 11: Pace — ending your chapter with a *bang!*

The same intrigue principle of the chapter's first line should also apply to the last line of your chapter. A last line should be like a thrilling goodnight kiss at the end of a first date, one that leaves you gasping and swaying on the threshold, unable to wait until you can see that person again.

Put as much thought and time into writing each chapter's last line as you put into your first.

Every scene contains conflict that will rise up and dip down constantly, so you need to end your chapter right at the peak of one of these high tension points. This will leave your reader needing to know which direction the path is about to go.

Author Example

The first chapter of *Dove* ends at a point where the characters have just realised they are in a whole world of trouble.

The car shuddered to a stop in a sunlit clearing as bright as the fear in Japhy's eyes. And all three frat boys turned to face me.

The word *shuddered* and the phrase *bright as fear* is used to incorporate again the theme of *fear* — which also ties in to the very first line of the chapter. The final sentence is an action, and a threatening one, so when the chapter ends the reader must continue on to find out what happens as a result.

If possible, make sure the last line of the chapter poses a new question. If you do this, your reader will continue onto the next chapter, and the one after that, and the one after that ...

Exercise: 15 min

1. On a sheet of paper, write out your entire last paragraph (or a few of them if they are short). In that

paragraph, circle three words or phrases that convey a sense of urgency, or intrigue. (If you can't find three, write down three words or phrases that convey for you a sense of urgency, and insert these into your last paragraph.)

2. During at least three separate points throughout your first chapter, insert these circled words/phrases again. Build each one into a paragraph that will further highlight the question, sense of urgency, or intrigue that will then build to a cliffhanger in your last paragraph.

Day Twenty: Symbolism

Symbols are used as an artistic way to keep your theme in the forefront of the reader's mind almost subconsciously.

Now that you know what your theme *is* you can use this to create a technique of flow and growth throughout your story, while implementing wonderful imagery and description by using a common recurring symbol.

Showing the different ways two characters view the exact same symbol is a great way to show diversity in your characters.

Showing the different ways one character views the same symbol at two points throughout their journey is a great way to show how they are changing.

Author Example

The symbolic metaphor used in *Dove* for the theme of freedom is a white feather: a symbol for peace, as well as for cowardice, which also brings up the conflicting emotions inherent in my main character. At one point, Ray and Japhy come across a mural showing a white feather in mid-fall above a pool of blood, (an image that ended up on the book cover). Ray looks at this more optimistically: the feather (Japhy) is safely frozen by the painting and will never land in the blood (war) below. Japhy, on the other hand, believes that no matter what happens, gravity is impossible to escape and the feather will have to land in the blood sooner or later.

Ray:
And on the wall opposite the large window was a mural: a single white feather, suspended in mid-fall, above a pool of glistening red blood. I stared at this painting. The details so crisp - each barb of the white feather so defined despite the same shade of white wall behind it. And even though this beautiful, pure entity seemed headed for that horrible, gory wetness below, it would never land, would never become stained in red, because it had been frozen in this moment. It was safe in this moment. And it would always be safe in this moment. No matter what.

Japhy:
I think about the mural on my bedroom wall. The way that feather falls, and will eventually be covered in blood. No matter what. [...] It doesn't matter what we do, it doesn't matter who we befriend, it doesn't matter where we hide; eventually, one way or another, we all end up covered in blood.

<u>Exercise: 15 min</u>

1. Consider your book's theme. Choose a symbol that can metaphorically represent this theme.

2. Write a scene in which two characters have differing views, and use this symbol as a metaphor to show their different beliefs.

Day Twenty-One: First Impressions Conclusion

You've made it to Day 21! This is an important milestone for you. According to science, if you have implemented writing into your routine every day for 21 days, you have made it a *habit*. They say now, if you continue this for a further 90 days, it will become a permanent lifestyle change.

This week we looked into how to up-level your first chapter by using different types of hooks. Creating a good hook for your story is imperative. By this point in the challenge, even if you weren't sure of your hook before starting, you will be now.

Your hook is based on your *theme*, which you worked out on Day 2.

Your hook is based on your character's *flaw*, which you worked out on Day 4.

Your hook is based on your character's internal *conflict*, which you worked out on Day 10.

Your hook is based on creating an unexpected *emotional reaction* in the reader, which you worked out on Day 12.

Your hook is based on your character's secret *backstory*, which you worked out on Day 18.

Exercise: 15 min

If you have a completed first chapter, read through it now and make sure it contains each of these hooks: theme, character flaw, conflict, emotion and backstory. If you discover a page with none of these, insert it.

If you are writing your first draft, write a first chapter outline that contains each of these hooks: theme, character flaw, conflict, emotion and backstory.

Day Twenty-Two: Introduction to Endings and What Now?

You've made it to our final week! I hope you have swaths of notes, scenes and chapters that you didn't have when we began this journey together. But even if you are only coming out of this challenge with a swirl of new ideas then that is great, too. I'm so proud of you for sticking it out, believing in yourself and making this a new daily habit.

Being a writer always seems exciting at the beginning, when you are first hit with that initial idea and spark and the accompanying surge of *need* to just get writing. You sit down and hammer out a few hundred words, or maybe a few thousand, but then slowly that inertia slows a little, the words stop coming, and you realise that this gig is *hard*. Crafting a piece of art that is 100,000 words long and needs to keep a reader invested for all of those 100,000 words is *hard*. Being a writer is *hard*.

But, just like childbirth, it is also worth it. Your book is worth it. Well done for believing in yourself and for sticking it out.

Today is all about believing in yourself. Today we are going to time travel. We are going into the quantum field.

Exercise: 5-10 min

Sit down and write a journal entry. Date it somewhere in the future, maybe in a year's time. Write about how great you feel because that thing you were dreaming of has just happened. Maybe you are holding your physical book in your hand, or you just signed a seven-book contract with a major publisher, or your book is being made into a movie, or you received a six-figure advance, or you finally typed those final words: *The End*.

Dream BIG, because big things *do* happen to other people, so why can't they happen to you? They *can*. Trust me.

The important thing is to put yourself in the skin of this future version of you. Feel the excitement. Don't just describe what you're doing, describe who you are *being*.

Try and continue this practice every day. Even if you don't do the journal entries, try and get into their skin once a day and live in that future version of you, feel it, be it, and believe that it is where you are heading.

Day Twenty-Three: Last Chapter

Today's work will depend on if you have already completed a first draft, and therefore have a final chapter written, or if you are still in the planning stages. Either one is fine, and you will get something out of it either way.

The best ending to a book is one that does not end when the last page does. If your characters live on in the reader's mind after the book is closed, then you have succeeded. If the reader keeps going over the elements in your story, thinking, "If only…", then you have succeeded. If the reader keeps thinking, "I wonder what will happen now…", then you have succeeded.

A great ending is something that a reader will not see coming, yet if they think back over the journey that they have just taken, they will notice a line of breadcrumbs leading them to this exact spot. When the ending arrives, they realise it was inevitable, no matter how unexpected it may have seemed.

Crafting a great ending is all about laying that trail of breadcrumbs. And the breadcrumbs are made out of — you guessed it — *theme*.

Start planning your final chapter, and final paragraph, early. If you are able to start thinking about where you are going, you can start to sprinkle little breadcrumbs through the manuscript. The last line needs to ring out as clear and lingering as a bell. If you can start working on it early, you will be able to give it the time and editing it needs to make it great. Or be able to go back once it's finished and sprinkle them in.

Exercise: 10 min

<u>Set a five minute timer</u>

Going back to the exercise from Day 6: Write a short paragraph about the book's theme. Why have you chosen this topic? Why is it important to you? Why should it be important to the reader? What do you want the reader to learn because of your book?

Rewrite these answers into a concluding scene. Would this work as a closing paragraph for your entire book?

Something that sums up the journey and leaves the reader with a feeling of inspiration that will stay with them even after they close the book.

Day Twenty-Four: Feedback

How are you at receiving feedback?

Sometimes we are so close to our work-in-progress we are too biased about it to consider someone else's opinion. Or we are too sensitive about our work that we are not willing to let anyone read it in the first place. These are not good mindsets to have.

Today, I want you to open your mind a little, thicken your skin a little, and do a little bit of research to find support groups in order to get feedback on your work.

The point of this is to get yourself used to receiving constructive criticism. Remember that criticism will ultimately help you to *improve* the manuscript somewhat, so look at this from the big picture. But also remember, this is only *one person's* opinion, so if it gets a bit too ouchy, feel free to just let it slide.

You don't have to implement every single suggestion, but you should at least *consider* it all. Even negative comments can help you improve — sometimes these are the most helpful.

<u>Exercise: 10 min</u>

If you are not already part of a writer's group, either a local in-person group, or an online one, take ten minutes right now to google around and make plans to join one.

If (and when) you are a member of a writer's group, I want you to send them something today that they can provide feedback on — whether it is your working title, character arc, plot outline, first chapter, or a general excerpt.

Once you have received your feedback, take some time to implement the suggestions given, *even if you don't agree*. Rework whatever it was you received feedback on, and then compare it to the original. You don't have to use the new version, but you do need to give it a chance.

Day Twenty-Five: Pitch

When I was submitting the *Dove* manuscript to agents and publishers, I had the frustrating experience of receiving this response from a literary agent:

Your manuscript is one of the best queries I have received to date. The characters are well defined and I immediately related to them and became lost in the tale. Brilliant work. I believe you have a very good chance of obtaining a publisher for this. Having said that, I feel that our agency would be unable to assist you at this time - in large part because I believe you are already doing a fantastic job of forwarding and promoting the manuscript yourself.

WTF, right? I mean, okay, yeah it is better to receive that response, than the usual, "Thanks, but no thanks," rejection letter. But seriously... to get so close but still be so far away was FRUSTRATING!

Today, we will look at writing a pitch that make agents and publishers grip your letter with white-knuckles, rather than dropping it onto the dreaded slush pile.

The pitch can be broken down into this simple template (Go back to Day 9 if you need a refresher on the 15 beats): (Protagonist), who has just (inciting incident), (fun and games) but when (the second inciting incident) happens he must learn (the theme) before (everything hits the fan).

<u>Author Example</u>

Dove pitch:
Japhy, a pacifist, who has just received his draft notice to the Vietnam War, hitches to Canada to escape army induction, but when the American Government closes in, he must learn that true freedom exists within the soul not without, before the war threatens to imprison him forever.

(*Fun fact:* I used this template to write out my pitch for this very 28 Day Challenge that you signed up for, so if you are reading this right now, then my template worked!)

28 Day Novel Writing Challenge Pitch:
A 28 Day Challenge for published or unpublished writers who are struggling to complete their novel's first draft, or need to up-level their existing MS. By signing up to this challenge, you will receive daily lessons and writing exercises around character development, story structure, first chapter, and publishing options. In these 28 days you will learn to make yourself and your writing a priority, carve out a daily routine that can become a habit, and lead you toward a completed Manuscript you will be proud of.

Exercise: 5 min

Use the pitch template to write out your book's pitch.

Protagonist: _________________

Core value: ___________________

Inciting incident: ______________________________

Fun and games: _____________________________

Second inciting incident: ________________________________

Theme: ________________

Everything hits the fan:

____

(Protagonist), who believes (core value), has just (inciting incident), and is now (fun and games), but when (the second inciting incident) happens he must learn (the theme) before (everything hits the fan).

Day Twenty-Six: Publishing Options

No one is too old or too young to get published.

But these days, a writer needs to decide on which publishing avenue to pursue: traditional or self publishing (also called Indie — ie. Independent).

Let's have a quick look at the pros and cons of self publishing and traditional publishing.

Profits (*pro — self publishing for royalties, but traditional may sell more books and offer an advance*).
With traditional publishing you might receive 10% of the royalties. With self publishing you can receive 75% of the royalties.

Creative control (*pro — self publishing*).
Traditional publishing will ask you to conform to their creative guidelines, which can mean editing the manuscript, book title and cover design. With self publishing the creative control stays with you.

Bookstores (*pro — traditional*).

Traditionally published books can end up in physical bookstores. Self-published books probably will not, unless you personally contact the stores and sell it to them.

Marketing (*pro — traditional*).
Marketing the book will be *your* responsibility no matter which path you choose. Granted, a traditional publisher might throw you a small marketing campaign, but unless you are Stephen King, it's not going to be huge.

Deadlines (*pro — self publishing*).
If you are self-published, then you work to your own schedule. If you are traditionally published then you work to theirs.

Rights (*pro — self publishing*).
If you sign to a traditional publisher, you sign over your rights. If you self-publish the copyright stays with you.

Speed (*pro — self publishing*).
With self publishing, your book can be online and available for purchase within 24 hours. Traditional publishing can take up to two years for your book to hit shelves.

Upfront cost (*pro — traditional*).
Traditional publishing will cover all costs associated with editing and printing your book. You are responsible for all costs involved in self publication.

The twenty-first century is both a great place for a writer to be, and a terrible place. Self publishing allows anyone to become a published author, selling their work with just the click of a button. This is great because it's easy. This is also not-so-great because there are now so many more books competing alongside yours, which means that yours really needs to stand out.

Self publishing can also come with a slight prejudice of being sub-par. For this reason, if you decide to take this path it is *so important* to hire a professional editor, and cover designer, and even a marketing team if you can, in order to make your work just as professional as books released by traditional publishing companies.

<u>Exercise: 15 min</u>

1. Make TWO pros and cons lists, one for traditional publishing, one for self publishing. Which one is going to work best for you?

2. Based on your decision, spend some time today researching your best publishing paths. For the traditional path, look up agents and publishers who are considering first timers, as well as places like *Allen and Unwin Australia's The Friday Pitch*, etc. that are willing to look at unsolicited manuscripts. For the self publishing path, spend some time today researching freelance editors, cover designers, etc.

3. Remember, no one is too old or too young to get published.

Day Twenty-Seven: Making Time

The most difficult part of being a writer, for me, is literally *being a writer*. I'm a mum of two young girls, and I run my own full-time business six days a week. Any free time I get where I'm not taking care of my clients, I'm taking care of my kids or slumped like a zombie beside my husband watching our latest show on Netflix. Therefore, I really had to think outside the square in order to be able to *write*, and *mum*, and *wife*, and *sleep*.

Start looking at your writing career as a *career*.

Schedule yourself time to write and stick to it. It is common when you have a busy schedule that writing is the thing that gets hit the hardest. Your writing time is usually deemed the least in importance when compared to a job that actually pays money, or spending quality time with your loved ones, or sleeping. If this is the case, schedule shorter blocks of time: fifteen minutes in the morning, fifteen minutes at night. Remember, even half an hour a day will equal three and a half hours of writing a week.

Working on your book doesn't have to mean a solid hour of typing and coming out with 2,000 words every time. It could mean sitting and thinking about your next plot twist, coming up with a better name for your lead character, or editing the page you wrote the day before.

If you can make a small amount of time every day, then it will become routine, habitual. And don't tell me you can't make some time for yourself, even just ten minutes… You've already been doing it all throughout this challenge, haven't you?

Prove to yourself that you are worth it and that you believe in yourself. Set aside time. You deserve it. If you can view your writing as an important part of your day, every day, then others will see it that way, too.

<u>Exercise: 15 min</u>

1. Pull up your calendar right now, and set aside some time every day to work on your book.

2. Work on your book in that allotted time *today*, and then every day.

Day Twenty-Eight: What Now?

It looks like you made it to the end. Well freaking done, my friend! I am so so *so* proud of you, and so honoured to have been a part of this month. It is my sincere hope that you have come away from this challenge with a substantial amount if words under your belt, and also a good healthy dose of inspiration to keep up the good work and keep moving forward on your writing journey.

You may be wondering, "So, now what?" Well, if you enjoyed completing this challenge, then I have a few other options for you.

If you want to continue the party, you can try out my other 28 Day Challenges and focus on a specific area of your work-in-progress.

28 Day *Creating Characters* Challenge
28 Day *Story Structure* Challenge
28 Day *First Impressions* Challenge
28 Day *Endings and What Now* Challenge

You are welcome to purchase the full course books and workbooks from which this month of bite-sized lessons and exercises were taken: *Novel Polishing* and *Novel Polishing Workbook*.

You can even choose to work with me one-on-one, either through manuscript assessments, editing, or as a book mentor. Contact me, or view my other books, at my website *M H Salter dot com*.

Thank you so much for taking the time to go on this journey with me.

Now, let me remind you that every great writer has something in common: *determination*.

The fact that you have put time and money into this challenge, and into yourself, proves that you *do* believe in yourself and you *are* determined to be a published writer.

<u>Exercise: 5 min</u>

1. Stand in front of a mirror and look yourself in the eyes. Place your hand on your heart and…

Make a promise to yourself that you will complete your novel.

Make a promise to yourself that you will carve out time for yourself.

Make a promise to yourself to just keep at it.

And make a promise to yourself to *believe that you are a great writer*.

2. Repeat step one of this exercise *every single day*.

First Chapter Assessment

Not 100% happy with your book's opening? Not sure why your first chapter isn't quite working? Get your chapter one assessment by M.H. Salter.

Receive an in-depth analysis on what is working well — and more importantly — on what is *not* working, with suggestions on how you can remedy and improve your first chapter.

- The analysis will focus on the first line and first paragraph, as well as the last line and last paragraph and how well these work together to bookend your first chapter.
- It will look at the different types of hooks you have used and how to add more, as well as the themes in your novel's beginning, and any symbols or motifs used in conjunction with this; if there don't seem to be any, you will receive some suggestions on what could work well throughout the manuscript.
- Conflict and pace will be analysed, both internal and external, and suggestions given on ways in which these can both be heightened.

- Prologues, or any use of backstory, will be highlighted to see if this could work better at a later point by enhancing tension in the lead-up to future revelations.

After receiving your assessment via email, you can dive even deeper by booking a one hour zoom call to discuss and brainstorm your novel further, or sign up to a one-on-one mentorship with M.H. Salter.

<u>What others had to say about their Chapter One Assessment:</u>

"I think it's a wonderful chance for writers to get that push in the right direction. I loved all of it."

"Melanie's assessment was warm and conveyed just how fully my first chapter had been read and understood. My novel was at a point where I knew it needed improving but I was out of ideas and inspiration about what to change. I now have, not only ideas, but concrete exercises to help me put those ideas into reality."

"I liked how the analysis was grouped beneath headings that corresponded to the [*Novel Polishing*] eBook. This made it much easier for me to see where the assessor was coming from, and pair it to the advice and activities in the [*Novel Polishing*] Book and Workbook. There was a good level of detail in the appraisal that left no question that my chapter had been thoroughly assessed. It would have been an apprehension of mine to have parted with my money and not received an appraisal that had taken the time to help me figure out exactly what my first chapter is (or should be) doing. So, thank you."

Book your Assessment with M.H. Salter now through *M H Salter dot com* or contact Melanie at *the dot excited dot writer dot is at gmail dot com dot A U.*